Auntie Kisha's Guide

What They Forgot to Tell You Before Your First Day of College.

Kisha S. White, M. Ed.

Copyright © 2022 by Kisha S. White

All rights reserved. No part of this publication may be reproduced, distributed, or transmitted in any form or by any means, including photocopying, recording, or other electronic or mechanical methods, without the prior written permission of the publisher, except in the case of brief quotations embodied in critical reviews and certain other noncommercial uses permitted by copyright law.

First Printing 2022
ISBN 9798843202293

Dedication

This book is dedicated to my forever loves, my children: Arie, Corey and Taylor.

3	WELCOME!
5	TIP#1: YOU DON'T KNOW WHAT YOU DON'T KNOW.
11	TIP#2: YOU ARE A NUMBER NEXT TO A NAME ON A LIST OF THOUSANDS OF FACELESS PEOPLE.
15	TIP#3: IF YOU THINK YOU'RE HEADED TOWARD A CLIFF, STOP!!!!
23	TIP#4: TAKE YOUR AZZ TO CLASS.
27	TIP#5: FINDING BALANCE IS THE NAME OF THE GAME.
31	TIP#6: ISOLATION DOES NOT EQUAL SUCCESS.
35	TIP#7: IT'S OKAY IF YOU DON'T HAVE IT ALL FIGURED OUT, BUT...
41	TIP#8: THE FRESHMAN-FIFTEEN IS NO MYTH.
47	TIP#9: ROOMMATES: CAN'T LIVE WITH THEM, CAN'T LIVE WITHOUT THEM?
52	TIP#10: TIME SEEMS TO BE SPEEDING AWAY!
56	CLOSING MESSAGE.

Notes:

Welcome!

It's crazy that almost 30 years after completing my undergrad degree, how much HASN'T changed? I saw it firsthand with my first two children, one a college grad and the other almost a college grad. In case you're wondering what I mean by this, many of the same things I experienced in college repeated themselves with my kids. When I think of all the things that adolescents face today when attending college for the first time, they are still about the same:

- Adjusting to being in new places.
- Learning how to juggle and balance life.
- Managing your finances.
- Taking care of your health and mental wellness.
- Receiving mentorship and guidance.

And my mantra still holds true: <u>If you don't ask questions, no one will be handing out answers.</u>

This book has been a labor of love. It's been in the making for about ten years. I created a guide that is easy to read and provides quick information for those considering attending college. I wanted it to be highly relatable, so I wrote it in my Auntie Kisha's voice, except without the colorful language. I used the same voice when discussing these last-minute items with my kids and their friends. Thus, I want to make sure you have a great understanding of precisely what you're getting into.

Please enjoy this journey. College can be the most fulfilling experience of your life. This is your time of discovery to find out exactly who you are and what you want from life. It's yours, and no one can ever change that fact.

xoxo xoxo,
Auntie Kisha

#1. YOU DON'T KNOW WHAT YOU DON'T KNOW.

You are ready! You will never be as prepared for the first day of school as you are right now! Then it happens. . .you find out you still have questions.

No matter how much preparation you've done, there will be some things you missed and some bits of information you don't know about.

You gotta know that's okay.

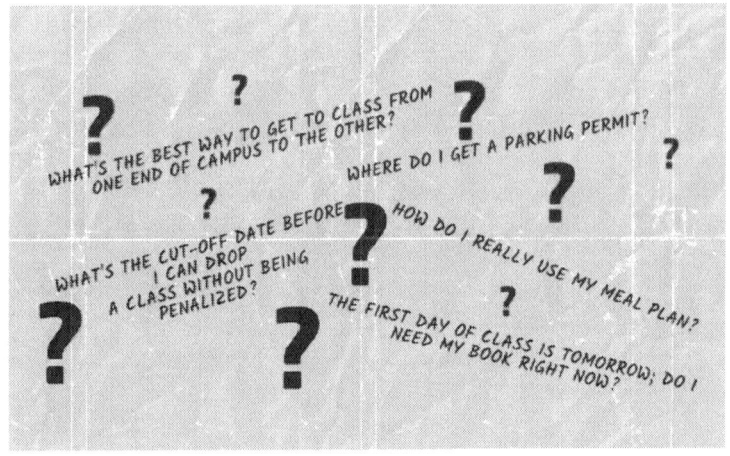

And trust, you will have many more questions as you go along.

Even if you're nervous and don't know whom to ask, ask anybody!

I bet these same people walking around looking like they have it all together probably don't or at one time definitely didn't.

ON TOP OF ALL OF THAT, YOU BETTER BELIEVE PEOPLE AREN'T GOING TO BE PASSING OUT FREE ANSWERS TO QUESTIONS YOU HAVEN'T EVEN ASKED YET.

Who cares if you look really silly in the process? You don't know?

SO YOU BETTER GET TO ASKING!

Ask all kinds of questions! And keep asking more questions!

The more information you have, the smarter you become, and the easier college gets.

Notes:

 # YOU ARE A NUMBER NEXT TO A NAME ON A LIST OF THOUSANDS OF FACELESS PEOPLE.

THIS IS GOING TO HURT A LITTLE, BUT YOU WILL THANK ME LATER.

Reality Check: I hate to say it, but you are not special to anyone on your campus except your folks and they don't live there!!

I'm sure you are unique, dynamic, and wonderful individuals, but do you know why?

BECAUSE NO ONE KNOWS YOU!!

In fact, unless you make yourself known, they don't particularly care.

The whole point is just that:

Make yourself known.

Get to know your professors and their graduate assistants. This is especially important if you find yourself on the struggle bus.

Find out the names of your department chair people for your major or for programs that may interest you.

Who is the President??? Better yet, who is the President's assistant?

Who is the Campus Dean of Students? Registrar? Dorm Resident Assistants?

These are just a few people that you may need to reach out to for assistance.

Differentiating yourself NOW from all the other names-on-the-list-of-faceless people will pay off big-time.

Notes:

Oh btw!

# #3. IF YOU THINK YOU'RE HEADED TOWARDS A CLIFF, STOP!!!!!!

Sometimes, you will face rough patches or dilemmas that may cause you to make decisions you normally wouldn't even consider.

Sometimes, you're going to feel you absolutely CAN overcome what looks like an "achievable hump" <u>all by yourself</u>. And you most definitely can!!! But, don't fool yourself, and don't be deceived! These seemingly "achievable humps," rough patches, or dilemmas are

CLIFFS.

Let's say you are driving down a stretch of highway. Suddenly you see a yellow caution sign: 20 miles-construction ahead. Then closer to the construction, the signs are bright orange, and the speed limit has changed from 70 to 50: detour 15 miles ahead. No

worries, you are still driving along and decide to continue forward (unadvisedly) past the detour. The signs that come along next are RED for STOP. DANGER. ROAD IS OUT. CLIFF AHEAD.
What are you going to do next???

College, for some of you, is your first time making real decisions on your own, but you don't have to go at it alone and you don't have anything to prove. So put your pride and egos away.

That means seeking help from parents, friends, mentors, professors, etc. Don't wait until you've driven all the way up to the cliff or off the cliff to think about pumping your breaks. It may be too late for your brakes to work properly. That's a scary situation!

What's even scarier is knowing that you could have asked for help or stopped before the situation became dire.

Here's a more straightforward example.

You were great in math in high school. You've enrolled in a trigonometry class, and it seems to be going great! Your homework is solid, and you think you have a pretty good understanding of what's happening.

Unfortunately, the grade you received on the first exam was TRASH! You just knew you aced that test! That's a potential

CLIFF.

Let's use the driving metaphor again and consider these possible options:

#1. You can start pumping the brakes now. That means you could drop the class if you feel unable to devote the time and effort to your studies.

#2. You can reach out NOW to your professors and classmates for help.

#3. What else can you do? Think of other ways to pump your brakes.

SEE HOW EASY IT WAS TO SLOW DOWN BEFORE YOU CRASHED?

Don't put yourself in any unnecessary situations by making things worse. Seek help when you need it and continue asking lots of questions.

Most of all,

be confident.

Trust your instincts.

Avoid driving over

CLIFFS.

#4. TAKE YOUR A22 TO CLASS.

This rule should have been #1. I don't care if you don't remember anything else from this book. I'm not here to get in your business about what you did the night before, how late you were up, or who you were with. Just promise me one thing.

Oh, you think that the professor won't miss you just because there are 200 or more other students in class?

Trust me!

Don't shrug off missing a class here or a class there. It's a big deal in the end when you find out the C you really needed to receive is pulled down to a D. Sorry!

Now you just wasted money, time, and more time and money because you have to retake that class. Was that really worth it??

Some professors are so picky about attendance that they offer students extra credit at the end of the semester to help pull their grades up. You show that you are more willing to establish a rapport with professors, assistants, and fellow students by attending class. And you become more engaged in class sessions.

Win-Win!

Notes:

Oh btw!

#5. FINDING BALANCE IS THE NAME OF THE GAME.

Unless high school was super hectic and you discovered how to manage it all, I bet you haven't figured out how to balance life quite yet.

IT'S NOT AS HARD AS YOU THINK. I PROMISE!

You literally have to take all these tips, mash them together, and TADA!!!!! Just go for what you know. It's more art than science.

Balance means prioritizing your schedule, making plans for the people you enjoy, making personal time for yourself, knowing when to buckle down in your studies, and knowing when it's time to take a step back and get recharged.

How well do you know yourself? Are you a morning person, a people person, a nightcrawler, a loner, a little bit of it all? Be true to yourself. Peer pressure will have you on 10 most of the time, pulling you to the east, west, north, and south. So stay focused on why you're there, to begin with, and not just to party!

Here's a scenario.

You're a nightcrawler. You come alive in the late afternoon and the evening. And that's when you get the most studying done.

Do you . . .

A. Schedule all your classes first thing in the morning.

B. Schedule all your classes online.

C. Schedule all your classes in the afternoon.

D. Who cares? I'm not going to class anyway. I'm just here to party.

If the above sounds like you, then don't schedule all your classes in the morning if you know you're not going to get up! Come on, Bruh!!!! Obviously, you want to fail!!

But if you want balance, you picked either b or c, right? cool!

#6. ISOLATION DOES NOT EQUAL SUCCESS.

By now, you've finally figured out that with everything going on, classes, people, professors, every now and then, you're gonna want to take a break. Cool! Take a break. Take time for yourself, but just remember one thing. Staying in chill mode for too long can be detrimental to your progress. Keeping yourself isolated from others is definitely not healthy. As humans, we need contact with others. That's why we gather in groups and seek out those with similar interests, values, and beliefs.

If you are struggling or not, someone is going through the same thing you are going through. It helps to have friends and mentors to speak with when times get bumpy.

REACH OUT! YOU COULD BE SAVING SOMEONE'S LIFE. YOU COULD BE SAVING YOUR OWN LIFE IN FACT.

If you don't think you are coping well, seek a counselor on campus. There are plenty of resources that can help. You don't have to suffer in silence and isolation.

Notes:

#7. IT'S OKAY IF YOU DON'T HAVE IT ALL FIGURED OUT, BUT...

THIS IS NOT THE SECTION SOME OF YOUR PARENTS WANT TO CO-SIGN.

Benjamin Franklin once stated, " By failing to prepare, you are preparing to fail." True or not, this statement isn't meant to discourage you. Instead, it's your reminder that everything you do should be purpose-driven--even if you don't have all the steps figured out just yet. Right now, your job is to receive an education and develop skills that will take you into your future.

But wait!! Believe it or not, your college experience is more than just about attending class and planning for your future career.

It's also about you discovering who you are and what you are made of.

And there are going to be plenty of people who think they have things all figured out. Celebrate and be happy for them!

But for those of you who are still trying to figure things out, you should be celebrating too! You better!!

YOU ARE NEVER GOING TO GET THIS TIME OF DISCOVERY AND CHANCE TO GROW UP EVER AGAIN!!!

There will be voices coming at you in all directions, maybe from your parents, siblings, friends, professors, counselors, and old teachers. But, the only voice that's really important is YOURS!

Don't ever be afraid of being unsure or changing your mind. Your process may seem like reckless abandonment to people looking a little too closely.

It's your journey. Own it! Don't fear it! Be flexible in accepting good advice. Be open when you seem to have missed an opportunity or two.

Also, don't forget about extracurricular activities. What are some causes you believe in? What are some things you are sincerely interested in studying on your own? Then, you can audit classes without spending any of your parent's hard-earned money.

Take things a day at a time by planning a little bit at a time and working on that plan. For example, maybe today, the goal is to earn the highest GPA possible. So even if you head in a different direction, you are already several steps ahead of the game.

You've just allowed doors to be opened and ready for your next big decision.

BECAUSE RIGHT NOW, IN THIS SPACE, IT'S OKAY NOT TO HAVE IT ALL FIGURED OUT.

Notes:

#8. THE "FRESHMAN-FIFTEEN" IS NO MYTH.

BEFORE YOU GO INTO THIS SECTION, LET ME TELL YOU THAT THIS HAS <u>ABSOLUTELY NOTHING</u> TO DO WITH FAT SHAMING OR MAKING ANYONE FEEL BAD ABOUT THEIR CURRENT WEIGHT, SIZE, OR BODY PROPORTIONS.

The freshman 15-pound weight gain is REAL! Late-night snacks, sleeping at odd times or not sleeping at all, not eating enough, or overeating! These are so real; before you know it, that weight has crept up on you. Brutal!!!

More than that, it's about all the things you may be doing to compensate for not feeling your best. For example, some people drink, smoke, overeat, or have risky sexual behaviors.

Sometimes gaining that "Freshman-15" is a pretty good indicator that some things in your life may require your attention. It's really about being aware of how you care for your body.

It's the only body you will have for a long time. Unless one of you geniuses figures out how to ethically clone humans or create humanoid avatars that will do all the work for us.

HA-HA-HA-HA-HA-HA!

WAIT! DON'T LAUGH. I SAW THE MOVIE.

This amounts to several factors we won't get into for this book. However, it's worth mentioning that you must find balance and figure out what's healthy for you.

HMM...

The truth is that once you enter college, life will be busy. Sometimes you feel your schedule is running you, and your professors are out to get you with all the homework you have to do. Surely they know this is not the only class you have? Of course, they do, but so what?

Take some time, sit down where it's quiet, and reflect. Then, you can use this inventory to help guide you.

QUICK check! INVENTORY

DISCLAIMER: This inventory is not meant to be a professional assessment. If you are having any mental or physical struggles, please see a mental health or medical practitioner immediately.

- How am I doing physically? Am I experiencing abnormal pains or bruises?
- How am I doing mentally?
- Am I tired?
- Have I been getting enough sleep?
- Are my skin, hair, and nails looking healthy?
- Have I had at least one bowel movement today?
- Have I had my period during the regular time? Was it the regular, normal amount? Was it heavier or lighter than usual? (if applicable)
- Have I been sexually active? Was it consensual? Was it protected?
- Have I noticed changes in my urination, discharge, or growths on my genitals?
- Have I been taking regular doses of prescribed medication?
- Have I gained or lost any weight?
- Am I eating regularly and selecting healthy options at least some times?
- Am I overeating or undereating?
- Am I drinking water?
- How is my mental state of mind or spiritual health?
- Am I talking to trusted people when I am sad, depressed, or stressed?

Notes:

#9. ROOMMATES: CAN'T LIVE <u>WITH</u> THEM. CAN'T LIVE <u>WITHOUT</u> THEM?

If given the opportunity, would you pick the roommate of your choice? Would you be brave and let the college or university pick for you?

Now is a perfect time if you ever want to test your ability to get along with anyone.

FOR ALL OF YOU WELL-INTENDING PEOPLE WHO DECIDED TO ROOM WITH A FRIEND OR SOMEONE FROM YOUR HOMETOWN, GOOD FOR YOU.

It shows that at least you did some planning and thought about what you thought would be the most comfortable and stress-free situation possible.

For all of you who decided to throw caution to the wind and play a little Russian Roulette, good for you too! Sometimes whom you end up rooming with is essentially out of your control. You don't know if you will get along with this person. Maybe you have similar interests. If they are a slob, and you are not, which may pose some problems. What if they have a different lifestyle, culture, or religion?

Before you fly off the handle and pack your stuff to leave, consider a few factors.

What do you have in common? Is it arts, general interests, reality TV, or sports? There are all sorts of things that people have in common.

Be flexible. Not everything is going to go your way all the time.

Be sure to set boundaries and establish rules for your living arrangement. Rules about studying, cleaning, having friends over.

These are just a few, but hopefully, you get the drift.

Notes:

#10. TIME SEEMS TO BE SPEEDING AWAY!

Before you realize it, you've gotten through college. But, of course, time is relative until you discover you've wasted a lot of yours. Graduation is now quickly upon you. But don't fret. Even though you can't gain the time back you think you have lost, you can make the most of the remaining time.

HERE ARE A FEW LAST-MINUTE THINGS YOU CAN DO TO MAKE THE MOST OF THE TIME LEFT.

1. <u>Get organized.</u> Once you clear your space of clutter, you usually clear your mind of clutter. It makes it much easier to make the best decisions.

2. <u>Join Professional Organizations.</u> Many professional organizations offer college students special rates or even free memberships when they sign up with their college email addresses. The great thing about joining professional organizations is that it gives you connections to mentors and a network in your field of study. Take advantage of it.

3. _Cut through the noise._ This is probably going to be the hardest part. So many well-intending people are going to want to give you unsolicited advice. Your job is to determine what you want and what is best for you.

4. _Talk with a mentor or advisor you trust._ Believe it or not, you are not alone, and the anxiety you feel today will eventually subside. Seek advice from people who genuinely support you and want the best for you.

5. _Face what's ahead with confidence._ During the last few years of your college experience, you will learn a lot about yourself, your values, and your beliefs. Please know that you would have done what few people will do. Yet, you have stuck to a long-term plan to complete your degree so face the future with confidence.

6. <u>Plan, plan, plan and plan some more.</u> Change can be challenging, but remember to create a plan. Your initial plan was to complete your degree. Use those skills you developed as the springboard to create a new plan. Create short-term and long-term goals. Stick to them, but be flexible and change what needs to be changed.

Hey!

You've made it through this book! I hope it provided just enough insight to help relieve some of your jitters about college and the bright future that lies before you. But, even if you decide college isn't for you or you think you need a gap year or two, I hope you take some of these tips and apply them to your current situation. Your Auntie Kisha is here for you: mean, life-worn, dramatic, and ready to give you that "look" when you need to straighten out a bit.

Enjoy the journey ahead and make every moment count!

xoxo xoxo,

Auntie Kisha

A Small Request

Thanks again for reading Auntie Kisha's Guide: What They Should Have Told You Before Your First Day of College. I have a quick favor to ask. Would you mind taking a minute or two and leaving an honest review for this book on Amazon? Reviews are the BEST way to help others purchase this book, and I check all my reviews, looking for helpful feedback.

Visit: www.coachkishawhite.com

Email me if you have any questions or want to tell me what you think. kwhite@coachkishawhite.com.

I'd love to hear from you!

Check out other published works by Coach Kisha White

Love
Heal
Create
2022 Self-reflection
Calendar & Planner

CLARITY
OF
INTENTION
Goalsetting Guide with
Calendar
2022

TAKE
ACTION
AND
CHANGE
FITNESS JOURNAL

Made in the USA
Columbia, SC
11 September 2022